Who Was
Pablo Picasso?

Who Was
Pablo Picasso?

Written and
illustrated by True Kelley

Grosset & Dunlap

With thanks to the public libraries
in Concord and Warner, New Hampshire—T.K.

GROSSET & DUNLAP
Published by the Penguin Group
Penguin Group (USA) Inc., 375 Hudson Street, New York, New York 10014, USA
Penguin Group (Canada), 90 Eglinton Avenue East, Suite 700,
Toronto, Ontario M4P 2Y3, Canada
(a division of Pearson Penguin Canada Inc.)
Penguin Books Ltd., 80 Strand, London WC2R 0RL, England
Penguin Group Ireland, 25 St. Stephen's Green, Dublin 2, Ireland
(a division of Penguin Books Ltd.)
Penguin Group (Australia), 250 Camberwell Road, Camberwell, Victoria 3124, Australia
(a division of Pearson Australia Group Pty. Ltd.)
Penguin Books India Pvt. Ltd., 11 Community Centre,
Panchsheel Park, New Delhi—110 017, India
Penguin Group (NZ), 67 Apollo Drive, Rosedale, North Shore 0632, New Zealand
(a division of Pearson New Zealand Ltd.)
Penguin Books (South Africa) (Pty.) Ltd., 24 Sturdee Avenue,
Rosebank, Johannesburg 2196, South Africa

Penguin Books Ltd., Registered Offices:
80 Strand, London WC2R 0RL, England

Library of Congress Control Number: 2009006096

ISBN 978-0-448-44987-6   20 19 18 17 16 15 14 13 12

Contents

Who Was
Pablo Picasso?

If you think about modern art, Picasso is probably the first name that pops into your head. Art today wouldn't be the same without him!

Pablo Picasso had a very long and interesting life. He lived through two world wars, the invention of electricity, telephones, radio and TV, movies, automobiles, and airplanes. As the world changed, he was able to change with it.

Picasso made all kinds of art and plenty of it. He worked hard every day for more than eighty years. Some people say he created 50,000 pieces of art! He must have had tons of energy.

He made paintings, posters, sculptures in stone and metal, ceramics, drawings, collages,

prints, poetry, theater sets, costumes, and more.
Picasso kept thinking of new ideas. He was
creative and skilled, but as soon as he mastered
a certain style, he'd move on. As a result, the
way he painted changed more than any other
great artist.

Unlike many artists, Picasso was successful and became famous quite quickly. He always knew how to attract attention. At nine years old, Picasso was selling his drawings. By the time he died at age ninety-one, he was the richest artist in history.

Through his art, Picasso sent powerful messages about politics, society, peace, and love. Because of Picasso, the dove is considered a symbol of peace. And his most famous painting, *Guernica*, shows the horror and brutality of war.

Picasso's art could be serious or playful, childlike or realistic, colorful or dark, simple or complex. When he was a child, he could draw as well as a talented grown-up. But the older he got, the more he wanted to make art like a child.

"Cat Catching a Bird," 1939

Chapter 1
The Boy Wonder

On October 25, 1881, in Malaga in southern Spain, an art teacher and his wife had a baby boy. They named him after many saints and relatives: Pablo Diego Jose Francisco de Paula Juan Nepomuceno Maria de los Remedios Cipriano de la Santisima Trinidad Ruiz y Picasso. Years later

Pablo's mother   Pablo's father

that baby became known as the great artist, Pablo Picasso. How would he ever have signed his whole name on a painting? It would have been impossible! So he just wrote "Picasso."

Pablo could draw before he could talk. His mother said his first words were "Piz! Piz!" That's baby talk in Spanish for *lapiz*, which means "pencil." When he was really little, he liked to draw spirals. He would sometimes draw pictures in the sand.

If he drew a horse, he could start from any point—the tail or the leg—and make a very good picture in one line. He could do the same with paper and scissors. Have you ever tried to do that? It's not easy!

Pablo's parents wanted him to be an artist. As a little boy, he often went to bullfights with his father. Pablo's first known painting was of a bullfight. He was only about eight years old when he did it. Everyone thought Pablo was an artistic genius—and they were right.

Pablo had two younger sisters, Lola and Conchita. Sadly, when Pablo was still young, seven-year-old Conchita died of diphtheria. The whole family was crushed. For the rest of his life, Pablo had a fear of death.

Conchita

Lola

When Pablo was thirteen, he had his first art show. By then, his father saw that Pablo painted better than he did. So Pablo's father gave his son all his brushes and paints and never painted again.

Pablo and his family moved to Barcelona, an exciting city full of artists. Pablo was accepted to the local art school where his father taught drawing. Even though he was only fourteen,

Pablo,
Age 15

Pablo skipped the basic courses and went right to the advanced ones. He amazed the teachers!

Pablo's career really began when he was sixteen. He did a painting called *Science and Charity*. His father and sister Lola were his models. Lola was shown sick in bed. Pablo's father posed as the doctor at her bedside. The painting was very realistic in style. It won a prize at an exhibit in Madrid. Pablo beat some of the best artists in Spain!

"Science and Charity," 1897

Pablo's family thought he had a great future as an artist. They sent him to Madrid to study art at the Royal Academy of San Fernando. It was supposed to be a good school, but Pablo skipped class a lot. His teachers wanted him to copy other paintings and statues. He thought this way of teaching was useless and old-fashioned.

He ended up spending a lot of time goofing off in cafés. He also loved going to the famous Prado Art Museum, where he saw the work of the Spanish masters El Greco and Francisco Goya.

PABLO'S LIFE IN SPAIN

PABLO AND HIS FAMILY MOVED FROM MALAGA IN SOUTHERN SPAIN, WHERE HE WAS BORN, TO LA CORUÑA IN NORTHERN SPAIN, AND THEN TO BARCELONA. AFTER THAT, PABLO WENT TO MADRID TO STUDY ART. WHEN HE BECAME SICK, HE WENT TO THE LITTLE VILLAGE OF HORTA DE SAN JUAN. HE LATER RETURNED TO BARCELONA, BUT HE COULDN'T RESIST PARIS.

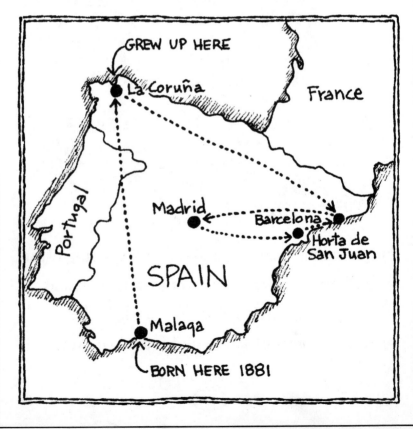

In the winter, Pablo came down with scarlet fever. He left school and stayed in a country village until he got better. He had a lot of time to think about his future. Pablo decided not to go back to school. He also decided that he wanted to paint his own way. His family was not going to like that, but Pablo was restless and ready to be on his own.

Chapter 2
The Young Artist

Pablo,
Age 18

Pablo moved back to Barcelona where he hung
out with a bunch of artists, poets, and writers at a
café called Els Quatre Gats ("The Four Cats").
They called themselves "Modernistes"—modern
artists. In 1900, Pablo had his first one-man show
at the café. There were more than fifty portraits
of friends and family and another sixty or so

drawings and paintings. One was a painting of a priest at the bedside of a dying woman. It was accepted for a show at the World's Fair in Paris. It was all Pablo needed as an excuse to move to Paris. An old art school friend, Carles Casagemas, went with him.

Carles and Pablo had no money. Their apartment had no furniture so Pablo painted furniture and bookcases on the walls. Then it didn't look so bare. He even painted a safe on the wall as if they had valuable things to put in it.

But the apartment didn't matter. They were in Paris! It was the center of the art and fashion world. Paris was full of life, and Picasso was full of energy! He was seeing the art of Monet, Degas, Cezanne, Van Gogh, Gauguin, and Toulouse-Lautrec. Paris was so colorful, and soon so were Pablo's paintings. For two months, he painted Paris scenes. He sold three pastels of bullfights. That was encouraging.

Pablo loved Paris. But poor Carles was broken-hearted. His girlfriend had left him. So Carles and Pablo moved back to Pablo's hometown in Spain. Pablo's family did not like what they saw when he walked in the door! The way he was dressed! And his long hair! They were sure he was wasting his life.

So Pablo moved to Madrid. He helped start an art magazine. He did political cartoons for the magazine about the sorry state of the poor. He left behind his friend Carles, who was still terribly depressed and difficult to be around.

Carles
Casagemas

Soon Carles Casagemas returned to Paris. He was at his wits' end. First he tried to shoot his old girlfriend. Then he shot himself and died.

Pablo was in shock. He may have also felt guilty about leaving his friend in such bad shape. Carles's death affected Picasso's painting. He painted two dark funeral scenes and two death portraits of Carles. Then he began painting with the color blue.

Pablo said, "It was thinking of Casagemas that made me start painting in blue." He did a self-portrait in 1901 that was mostly in blues. It made him look very sad. Later, this time became known as Picasso's Blue Period.

"Self-portrait with Cloak," 1901

From 1901 to 1904, Pablo moved back and forth between Barcelona and Paris. He lived in cheap hotel rooms and run-down apartments. Pablo shared one apartment with Max Jacob, a poet. They could only afford one bed, so Pablo slept in it during the day, and Max slept in it at night. Pablo worked at night, a habit that continued for the rest of his life.

Because he often couldn't afford to buy canvases and paints, Pablo did lots of drawings. His subjects were beggars, blind people, lonely people, and prisoners. Pablo cared about these people. For models, he visited a women's prison in Paris. All his life, Pablo loved painting women.

It was 1903. In only a little over a year, Pablo did fifty paintings using tones of blue and green. No one bought them. People didn't want to put such depressing pictures on their walls. Pablo's dad and a lot of his friends were sure Pablo was headed in the wrong direction with

his strange blue paintings. But did Pablo listen?
No. He did what he wanted!

"The Old Guitarist," 1903
(in shades of blue)

Chapter 3
Life in Paris

Picasso, 1904

What made Pablo snap out of his Blue Period? Moving back to Paris—this time for good—was one cause. Lively Paris worked its magic on Pablo. He became happier. He started doing colorful paintings of jugglers and acrobats in a traveling circus. They were all outsiders to society, just like the people he had painted in his Blue Period.

LES SALTIMBANQUES

PABLO WORKED HARD ON HIS PAINTING, *LES SALTIMBANQUES* (THE FAMILY OF ACROBATS). HE USED BOTH FERNANDE AND A FRIEND AS MODELS FOR THE CIRCUS FAMILY. X-RAY STUDIES OF THE PAINTING SHOW THAT HE DID THE PAINTING COMPLETELY OVER FOUR TIMES UNTIL HE HAD IT THE WAY HE WANTED.

The other reason that his Blue Period ended was Pablo had a new girlfriend. She was a beautiful artist named Fernande Olivier. His

Fernande and Pablo with their dogs, 1906

happiness showed in his paintings. This time in Pablo's life is sometimes called the Rose Period, but his paintings had many colors. Not just pinks.

PICASSO'S PETS

THROUGHOUT HIS LIFE, PABLO HAD MANY PETS, INCLUDING A TAME WHITE MOUSE, A TORTOISE, A GOAT, AND A MONKEY. HE WAS A TRUE DOG LOVER. WHEN HE WAS STILL A STRUGGLING ARTIST, HE HAD A BIG, SWEET, OLD DOG NAMED FRIKA. ONCE WHEN PABLO HAD NO FOOD, FRIKA TROTTED IN DRAGGING A STRING OF SAUSAGES! HIS ALL-TIME FAVORITE PET WAS PROBABLY A DACHSHUND NAMED LUMP. LUMP MEANS "RASCAL" IN GERMAN. PABLO PAINTED LUMP INTO HIS COPY OF *LAS MENINAS* INSTEAD OF THE NOBLE-LOOKING HOUND THAT VALASQUEZ PAINTED IN THE ORIGINAL.

Esmerelda

Yan

Gat

Kasbek

Lump

Pablo and Fernande lived in a big, run-down apartment building that was full of artists and poets. Their room was damp and a mess with lots of projects going on. Pablo didn't like to throw out anything. He said, "Why should you want me to throw away what has done me the favor of coming into my hands?"

They had a big, yellow dog named Frika, and they kept a pet white mouse in a dresser drawer. Pablo liked to work at night by oil lamp. He often worked until five or six in the morning. In winter, the room was sometimes so cold that leftover cups of tea froze overnight.

Around this time, Pablo was meeting lots of interesting people in Paris. They thought he was interesting, too. He was intense and complicated. He could be very charming and his curiosity, energy, intellect, and originality caught people's

Picasso with friends in a café

attention. Despite being short, only five feet
three inches tall, he was very striking-looking
with piercing black eyes.

He met a rich American woman named
Gertrude Stein and her brother Leo. Gertrude

Leo Stein   Gertrude Stein

was a poet. She had written the famous line,
"Rose is a rose is a rose." She was one of the first
people to really appreciate Pablo's paintings, and
she bought some of them.

Poets and artists met at the Steins's house in Paris on Saturday nights. Pablo met the painter Henri Matisse there. Pablo thought Matisse was the greatest painter of the time. "All things considered, there is only Matisse," he once said. Even though they were competitors, they became lifelong friends.

Matisse, Gertrude Stein, and Picasso in Paris

PORTRAIT OF GERTRUDE STEIN

IN 1906, PABLO WORKED ON A PORTRAIT OF
GERTRUDE. IT WAS TORTURE FOR PABLO BECAUSE
HE JUST COULDN'T GET HER FACE RIGHT. SHE SAT
FOR THE PORTRAIT EIGHTY TIMES! IT PROBABLY
WAS TORTURE FOR GERTRUDE, TOO! PABLO
GAVE UP FOR THE SUMMER; IN THE FALL, HE
PAINTED IN HER FACE FROM MEMORY. IT LOOKED
LIKE A PRIMITIVE MASK. PABLO HAD BEEN LOOKING
AT AFRICAN AND PRIMITIVE ART IN A MUSEUM,
WHICH EXPLAINS WHY. HE WAS NEVER AFRAID
TO BORROW IDEAS.

A wooden African mask

A primitive Iberian sculpture

PEOPLE DIDN'T THINK THE PAINTING
LOOKED LIKE GERTRUDE AT ALL, BUT SHE
LOVED IT. SHE SAID, "FOR ME, IT IS I."

After working on a portrait of Gertrude Stein, Pablo realized that he didn't have to paint exactly what he saw. He could paint what he imagined. This led to a turning point for Pablo. It was a turning point in the history of modern art!

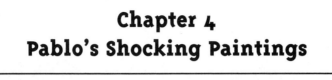

Chapter 4
Pablo's Shocking Paintings

In 1907, Pablo painted the biggest painting he had ever done: eight feet tall and eight feet wide. It showed five women, one whose head looked like it was on backward. The painting was called *Les Demoiselles D'Avignon*.

LES DEMOISELLES D'AVIGNON

THE PAINTING WAS REALLY WILD BY THE STANDARDS OF THE DAY. THE FIVE WOMEN IN THE PAINTING LOOK VERY ANGULAR AND DISTORTED. THEY ARE UGLY! THEY SEEM TO BE BREAKING INTO PIECES.

PEOPLE THOUGHT THE PAINTING SHOULD LOOK MORE REAL. THIS WAS UPSETTING! SHOCKING! NO ONE HAD EVER DONE A PAINTING LIKE IT. CREATING IT CHANGED PABLO'S UNDERSTANDING OF PAINTING. PABLO HAD TAKEN MANY MONTHS TO PAINT THIS PICTURE. HE HAD DONE MANY, MANY SKETCHES FOR IT (EIGHT HUNDRED AND NINE!). HE KNEW HE WAS BREAKING ALL THE RULES, BUT HE WAS TRYING TO PAINT THE WOMEN FROM MORE THAN ONE ANGLE AT A TIME AS IF THE VIEWER WAS SEEING THEM FROM MANY DIFFERENT SIDES ALL AT ONCE.

African Tribal Mask

Picasso Woman

Everyone hated it! One critic said it was "the work of a madman." Pablo put it away and didn't show it again for nine years. It was fun to get the attention, but his feelings were hurt.

Today it has been called the first modern twentieth century painting. Picasso had found a new way of seeing.

There was one person who really liked Pablo's experimental style. He was an art gallery owner named D. H. Kahnweiler. He became Pablo's art dealer and close friend.

D. H. Kahnweiler

Another close friend was the artist Georges Braque. Picasso and Braque found that they thought alike.

Georges Braque

They were both influenced by the paintings of Paul Cezanne.

"The Sea at L'Estaques" by Paul Cezanne

For five years, Braque and Picasso saw each other every day. They even went on vacation together. They worked together so closely that Pablo said, at times, they couldn't tell who had painted which painting. They would also look at each other's work and decide together if a painting was finished. Braque said he and Picasso were like mountain climbers attached to the same rope. Pablo never again worked so closely with another artist.

Braque and Picasso did still life paintings, landscapes, and portraits. They both used only a few colors and broke up objects in the paintings into cubes and geometric shapes. They were trying to paint their subjects from all sides at once. Pablo said, "I paint objects as I think them, not as I see them." Together, they were inventing a new style—cubism!

"Portrait of Ambroise Vollard," 1910

Of all the important artwork that Pablo created in his life, it was cubism that made him famous. At first people were shocked by cubism. They had never seen anything like it. But soon people realized they liked it!

Pablo said, "I knew we were painting strange things, but the world seemed a strange place to us."

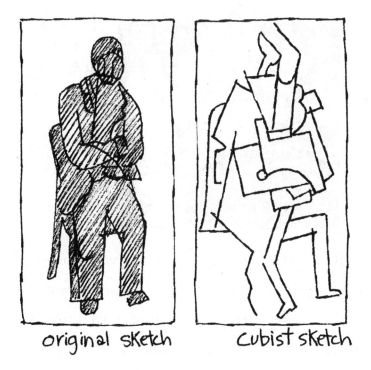

original sketch   cubist sketch

Chapter 5
Something New

Picasso,
1907,
age 26

By 1909, Pablo was becoming well-known.
His paintings were different, but people were
buying them. He and Fernande moved into a
fancier house. They hired a maid. They spent
the summer with Braque in an old villa in the

Fernande
Olivier

mountains. Then he and Fernande broke up.
Pablo said, "Her beauty held me, but I could
not stand any of her little
ways."

Soon Pablo had a new
girlfriend, Eva Gouel.
Pablo painted a picture

Eva Gouel

of Eva, called *Ma Jolie*, which means "My Pretty Girl." Pablo was in love again. He fell in love many times in his long life.

"Ma Jolie," 1912

Once again Picasso and Braque were on to something new. They started using stencils and printed words in their paintings. They also began pasting things on to their pictures. If they wanted a newspaper to be shown, instead of painting it, they stuck on a real piece of newspaper. That was how collage began. Collage means "to stick." One of Pablo's first collages was called *Still Life with Chair Caning.*

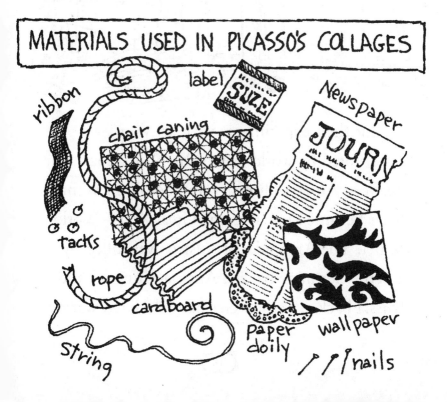

MATERIALS USED IN PICASSO'S COLLAGES

ribbon

label SUZE

Newspaper

chair caning

JOURN

tacks

rope

cardboard

string

paper doily

wallpaper

nails

Braque and Picasso went on, in their playful way, sticking other things onto their paintings—pieces of cloth, sandpaper, wallpaper, even trash!

But their experiments with art were interrupted by world events. In 1914, a local war between Austria-Hungary and Serbia grew into what became known as the Great War—World War I. The Archduke of Austria was killed by a Serb. Germany backed Austria-Hungary and Russia backed Serbia. Germany declared war on

Russia, and then on France. Soon countries all over the world were involved, including the United States.

In 1914, Braque was drafted into the French army. Pablo wasn't a French citizen. He didn't have to join the army. He stayed in Paris while many of his friends went off to fight. Pablo missed them.

France was fighting against Germany. Because Pablo's friend, the gallery owner Kahnweiler, was German, he was forced to leave France. (The French thought anybody German was an enemy.) The gallery was closed by the French authorities. All of Pablo's work there was confiscated.

In 1915 Pablo's dear Eva died of tuberculosis. Pablo was brokenhearted. Again his sadness showed in his paintings. He had worked on one painting while Eva was sick, *Harlequin*, and finished it after she died. It shows a clownlike artist in front of an easel holding an unfinished

painting. The background is black. It was a
bleak time in Europe and in Pablo's personal life
as well.

Chapter 6
Falling in Love Again and Again

Picasso, Age 36, 1917

During World War I, Pablo found some new friends in Paris. One of them was a poet and playwright named Jean Cocteau. He introduced Pablo to a music composer. The two of them convinced Pablo to design a set and costumes for a ballet to be performed in Rome. It was about a circus and was called *Parade*. Pablo had never even seen a ballet before! He traveled to

Rome to work on it. When it was finally performed, *Parade* bombed. It was too different for most people. The costumes were wild.

Ballet Dancers!

The French Manager Costume

The American Manager Costume

So were the sets . . . and the music . . . and the dancing.

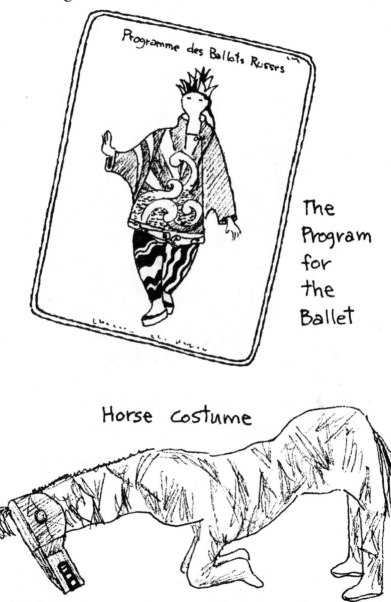

Programme des Ballets Russes

The Program for the Ballet

Horse Costume

"Olga," 1917

While in Rome, Pablo became fascinated with ancient Greek and Roman art. He also became fascinated with beautiful Olga Khokhlova, one of the dancers in the ballet. He married her a year later.

Back in Paris, Olga introduced Pablo to high society. They went to formal balls and to fancy resorts. For someone like Pablo who had always cared so much about the poor, this was quite a switch. Olga was a snob. She kept Picasso away from old friends, and Pablo went along with it.

Picasso and Olga at a fancy ball in the 1920s

He didn't need to work anymore. He was already rich. Yet that didn't mean he stopped working. Once again, he just changed direction.

After the war, Pablo did far less with cubism and collage. He went back to painting in more traditional ways. After all his experimenting, Pablo had found another way to surprise people . . . by not being the Picasso they expected!

In 1921, Pablo and Olga had a son, Paulo. Pablo adored his new baby. He loved being a father, but it was a big change for him.

Paulo, age 2

Over and over he painted mother and son in a new style. The forms were solid-looking, not jagged and broken as in his cubist paintings.

His painting, *Three Women at the Spring*, shows three figures in classical Greek style clothing. They have very rounded forms and thick legs. Picasso said painting the legs brought back childhood memories of crawling under the dinner table and seeing his aunts' ankles.

At the same time he also painted *Three Musicians* in a very simplified cubist style. But now the shapes and colors were brighter. The figures looked like pieces in a jigsaw puzzle. Why would Picasso change suddenly from one style to another? He said he was simply using the style that best suited the subject.

Picasso in his studio, 1919

Then Pablo started painting things like centaurs and fauns. He had admired them in the ancient statues and art that he had seen in Italy.

Centaur

Faun

The cubists thought Picasso was selling out. Picasso didn't care what other artists thought. He didn't want to be labeled. He was Picasso!

By 1925, Picasso became interested in the surrealist movement in art and literature. Surrealist painting was a way of expressing the unconscious mind.

"Woman in Red Armchair," 1932

Picasso painted a world of dreams and nightmares. He took part in a show of surrealist art. On the side, Picasso was also writing poetry and doing book illustrations and etchings. He had enough energy for ten people!

Many of Picasso's surrealistic drawings and etchings were about bullfighting. He also made many images of the Minotaur, an imaginary creature that was half man and half bull. Some art critics think that Picasso liked to think of himself as a Minotaur!

Minotaur

MAKING AN ETCHING

ETCHINGS ARE DRAWINGS SCRATCHED WITH A SHARP TOOL ON A METAL PLATE. PRINTS ARE THEN MADE FROM THE PLATE.

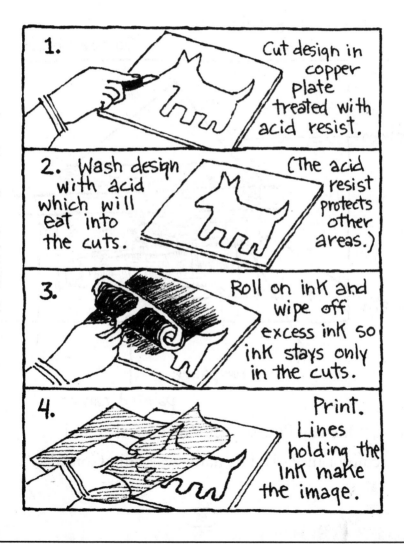

1. Cut design in copper plate treated with acid resist.

2. Wash design with acid which will eat into the cuts. (The acid resist protects other areas.)

3. Roll on ink and wipe off excess ink so ink stays only in the cuts.

4. Print. Lines holding the ink make the image.

Picasso also became interested in making sculpture. He had done some collage paintings of a guitar that used many 3-D objects—nails, string, and a cloth. It was as if paintings like this were becoming sculptures.

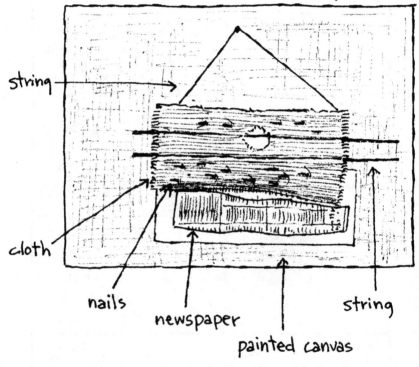

"Guitar," 1926

string

cloth

nails

newspaper

painted canvas

string

One day Picasso met a metalworker and sculptor in Paris. His name was Julio Gonzales.

He was Spanish, too. Julio and Pablo became
friends. They worked together on abstract
sculptures using welded metal rods and wire.
It was something completely new.

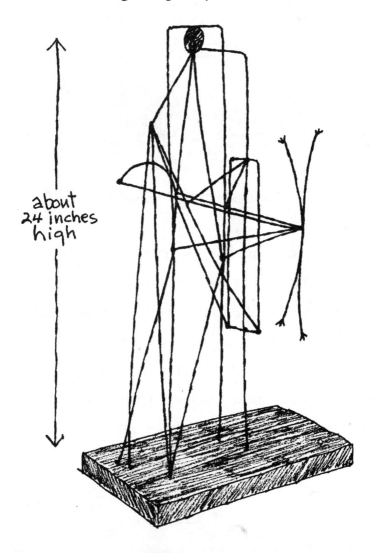

about
24 inches
high

Picasso's messy studio, 1920

Unfortunately, Pablo's marriage to Olga was falling apart. They were living on separate floors of their house. She hated his messy studio (and it was messy!). Pablo said the mess inspired him. Olga was the problem. "She asked too much of me," he said. So he bought a grand house north of Paris to escape her. Picasso said his last months with Olga were a nightmare.

At his new place Picasso set up a sculpture studio in the stables. He made big plaster heads and started doing sculpture made with odd materials. One sculpture, *Head of a Woman*, was made using colanders.

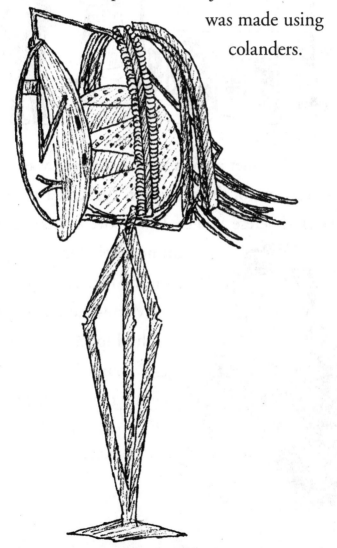

Picasso met a young girl just as she was coming out of the subway in Paris. Her name was Marie-Therese Walter. It was love at first sight.

Immediately Picasso began painting her. Years later, he and Marie-Therese had a child together, a girl named Maya. Did they live happily ever after? No!

Dora
Maar,
1936

Picasso met a photographer named Dora
Maar. He fell in love with her just a year after
his daughter was born. Picasso seemed to enjoy
having a very complicated love life. He was still
seeing Marie-Therese and still dealing with Olga,
and now there was Dora.

PICASSO'S MUSES ... THE WOMEN IN HIS LIFE

WOMEN WERE ATTRACTED TO PICASSO, BUT HE
MUST HAVE BEEN DIFFICULT TO LIVE WITH! HE HAD
A TEMPER AND COULD BE GRUMPY WHEN HIS WORK
WASN'T GOING WELL. OF COURSE, HE WAS TOTALLY
CHARMING AT OTHER TIMES. HE LOVED WOMEN, BUT
HE WAS VERY SELF-CENTERED AND ABSORBED BY

MET FERNANDE
IN 1904

MET EVA
IN 1911

MET OLGA
IN 1917

MET MARIE
THERESE
IN 1927

SON PAULO,
BORN 1921

DAUGHTER MAYA,
BORN 1935

HIS ART. IN HIS LIFE HE HAD MANY GIRLFRIENDS AND WIVES, AND FOUR CHILDREN. THEY WERE IMPORTANT TO HIM AS MODELS AND AS HIS GREATEST SOURCE OF INSPIRATION. WE KNOW WHAT THE WOMEN LOOKED LIKE BECAUSE HE DREW AND PAINTED THEM ALL. THEY WERE ALL BEAUTIFUL.

MET DORA
IN 1936

MET FRANÇOISE
IN 1944

MET JACQUELINE
IN 1953

SON CLAUDE,
BORN 1947

DAUGHTER PALOMA,
BORN 1949

Chapter 7
War and Peace

Some artists work on one idea and in one style. But Picasso changed all the time. Picasso's paintings reflected what was going on in his personal life as well as what was happening in the outside world.

In 1936 the Spanish Civil War broke out. Picasso was living in Paris, yet he was deeply affected by the war in Spain. He was a Spaniard, after all.

In Spain, a Republican government had been elected. But it was overthrown by General Francisco Franco and his forces. Franco was a dictator and ruled Spain until his death in 1975. Because of Franco, Picasso never returned to his native country.

General
Franco

In April, 1937, the town of Guernica in northeast Spain was bombed by the Germans who were helping Franco and his men. Guernica was not far from where Picasso grew up. The bombs fell on market day. More than sixteen hundred people—men, women, and children—were killed. Almost nine hundred more were injured. There was no military reason for the attack.

Picasso was outraged by the murder of all these

innocent people. With all his passion, he painted a huge twelve-foot-high-by-twenty-six-foot-long painting called *Guernica*. It is his most famous painting. He finished it in just three weeks. His new girlfriend, Dora, took many photographs of him working on it.

In gray tones, the painting shows a screaming horse, a fallen soldier, a screaming woman on fire falling from a burning house, and a mother holding her dead baby. There's a cutoff arm holding a sword and a severed head. There is a bull amid the chaos, which may symbolize the hope of overcoming Franco. *Guernica* is a very strong and disturbing portrayal of the horrors of war.

When he was asked to explain the painting, Picasso said, "It isn't up to the painter to define the symbols. Otherwise, it would be better if he wrote them out in so many words!"

Then, in 1939, World War II started after the German army invaded Poland. Fearing bombings, museums in Paris closed down. Much of the art was moved and hidden in the countryside. Many artists fled the city. So did Picasso with his family. They moved to Royan, a small town in France on the Atlantic coast.

In 1940, the Germans occupied Paris. Picasso decided to move back to his studio there. Why? Perhaps Picasso hoped his presence would be a proud symbol to the French of defiance and freedom.

It was hard to get food. So sometimes Picasso painted pictures of sausages and leeks. Art supplies were also scarce. Even so, Picasso managed to paint every day. He also wrote a play. The Nazis did not approve of any of his work. But that didn't stop Picasso!

Picasso's love for Dora was fading. He met a young artist, Françoise Gilot, and began a ten-year-long romance with her.

In 1944, the Nazis were finally driven out of Paris. Picasso kept on painting. He sang loudly while he worked to drown out the sounds of the gunfire. As soon as the Germans were gone, Paris had a party. The city was free again. The war was almost over.

Françoise Gilot, 1943

American soldiers poured into Paris. Some said the two things they most wanted to do were see the Eiffel Tower and meet Picasso! Picasso was pleased to give tours of his studio. Everyone was welcome. Some soldiers arrived so tired, they fell asleep there. Once someone counted twenty sleeping men in the studio!

American troops march into liberated Paris.

The second World War lasted six years. Picasso had now lived through three wars. He knew how important it was to work for peace. In 1948, he went to the Peace Congress in Poland. The following year, he made a poster of a dove for the Peace Congress. Because of Picasso, the dove has become a symbol for peace all over the world.

Chapter 8
Pots and Pans

Picasso, 1955

After the war, Picasso and Françoise moved to the town of Vallauris in southern France. They lived in an old perfume factory with room for a sculpture studio. Their two children were born in Vallauris—a son, Claude, in 1947 and a

Picasso and Françoise
with their children,
Claude and Paloma, in 1952

daughter, Paloma (which means "dove"), in 1949.

There was also a pottery factory in town.
Picasso began working with the potters, making
and decorating ceramics, plates, and vases.

At first he just decorated pieces made by the
potters. But soon he was making pottery himself.
His designs were happy and playful.

At home in his studio, Picasso worked on amusing and childlike sculptures. They were made from things he found around the place. And so the pieces were called "Found Art." At a junkyard, Picasso saw a bicycle seat and handlebars lying next to each other. He welded them together. Suddenly they looked exactly like a bull's head!

"Bull's Head," 1943

For a sculpture of a woman pushing a baby carriage, Picasso used parts from a real baby carriage and cake pans.

"Woman with Baby Carriage," 1950

Some of his sculptures would make you laugh. For an ape, Picasso used a toy car for a face, a car spring for a tail, a jug for a body, and coffee cup handles for ears.

"The Ape and Her Young," 1952

"Goat," 1950 (cast 1952)

He made a sculpture of a goat out of flowerpots, a basket, and palm leaves.

Pablo was now a happy family man. He spent time with his children, teaching them to swim, playing, and drawing with them. He seemed to have found peace in his life. But did it last? No!

Picasso, Claude, and Paloma

Chapter 9
Busy to the End

In the studio around 1950

In 1953, when Picasso was seventy-one years old, Françoise left him. He couldn't believe it!

No woman had ever left him before. He had always been the one to call it quits. Françoise took the children with her. That was a huge blow to Pablo. His friend, the artist Henri Matisse, died a little while later. Another blow.

But leave it to Picasso to find romance again! He met a woman, Jacqueline Roque, at the pottery factory. She was devoted to him until the

day he died. They got married when Pablo was eighty years old! Pablo and Jacqueline lived in luxurious houses in southern France. Picasso

painted pictures of his studio and of Jacqueline.
He did at least one hundred and fifty portraits of
her. He did a group of pictures called "The Artist
and Model Series." He kept experimenting and
exploring. Picasso said, "I have less and less time
and yet, I have more and more to say."

One of his projects was to look at old
masterpieces by other artists, such as the Spanish
painter Velazquez, and translate the paintings into

his own style. Picasso seemed to be trying to understand the history of art by redoing it in his own way.

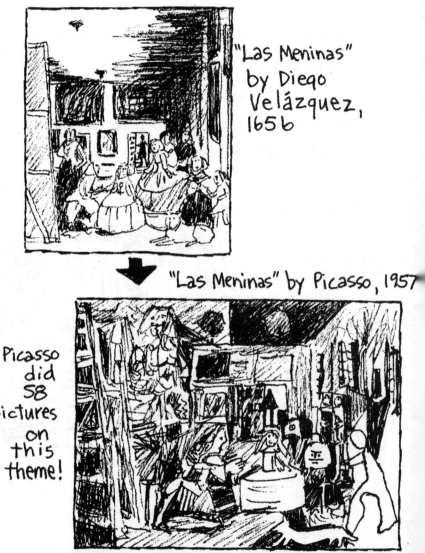

"Las Meninas" by Diego Velázquez, 1656

"Las Meninas" by Picasso, 1957

Picasso did 58 pictures on this theme!

By now there were shows of his art all over the world. He was such a celebrity that it was hard to have any privacy. He and Jacqueline moved to a secluded villa in the hills of southern France. His villa had electronic gates and guard dogs. Even his own children had trouble getting in to see him.

On his eighty-fifth birthday, museums in Paris honored Picasso with shows of his work—a thousand pieces in all.

And still Picasso kept working. Even at ninety-one he was experimenting. He started making linoleum block prints.

"The Footballer," 1961

sheet metal sculpture, 15 feet tall

He also made a new kind of sculpture with painted sheet metal. He would still turn out three, four, or even five paintings a day!

Sometimes it seemed as if Picasso would go on

HOW TO MAKE A LINOLEUM BLOCK PRINT

1. Draw your design <u>in reverse</u> on a linoleum block.

2. Carve <u>around</u> your lines removing all linoleum where you want the color of the paper you print on.

3. Roll ink on block with a brayer or roller.

4. Place paper over block. Rub with a plastic spoon.

VOILA!

forever. However, on April 8, 1973, Pablo Picasso's heart finally gave out. The doctor by his bedside heard his last words: "You are wrong not to be married. It's useful." That was Picasso, surprising to the end.

Several museums are now devoted to his art—including one in Barcelona and one in Paris.

He left behind a huge body of work. There may be as many as fifty thousand pieces. But it is not the quantity of art that boggles the mind. It is his genius that is so amazing. How could one man have so much energy? How could one man come up with so many new ideas? How could one man have lived so fully? Picasso's gift to the world was his art, but he also showed how a creative life could be when lived with energy, originality, and passion.

WHAT PICASSO PRODUCED, AGED 88-91!

1969 . . .

165 OIL PAINTINGS AND ... 45 DRAWINGS

1970 TO MARCH 1972 . . .

156 ENGRAVINGS

1970 . . .

194 DRAWINGS

NOVEMBER 1971 TO AUGUST 1972 . . .

172 DRAWINGS

SEPTEMBER 1970 TO JUNE 1972 . . .

201 PAINTINGS

Picasso's last self-portrait,
1972

TIMELINE OF PABLO PICASSO'S LIFE

1881	Born October 25
1889	Paints first oil painting, age eight
1895	Moves to Barcelona and goes to School of Fine Arts
1900	First show at Els Quatre Gats Café
1901	Casegemas dies; Blue Period begins; Moves back and forth between Spain and France, 1901-1904
1906	Paints *Gertrude Stein*; meets Matisse and Braque
1912	First collages
1921	Son Paulo born to wife Olga Khokhlova
1925	First surrealist show
1937	Paints *Guernica*
1947	Son Claude born to Françoise Gilot; begins making ceramics
1949	Invents dove as peace symbol; daughter Paloma born to Françoise
1954	Matisse dies
1961	Marries Jacqueline; makes corrugated metal sculptures
1966	One thousand works are shown in Paris for Picasso's eighty-fifth birthday
1973	Dies April 8, age ninety-one

TIMELINE OF THE WORLD

Albert Einstein is born	1879
World's Fair in Paris	1900
Wright brothers fly a plane at Kitty Hawk, North Carolina	1903
The *Titanic* sinks on its very first voyage on April 14	1912
World War I starts	1914
World War I ends; Great influenza epidemic kills an estimated 20-40 million people around the world	1918
The New York stock market crashes, setting off the Great Depression	1929
Adolf Hitler becomes chancellor of Nazi Germany	1933
Spanish Civil War begins and lasts for three years	1936
World War II begins	1939
United States drops atomic bombs on two Japanese cities; World War II ends	1945
Elvis Presley has his first number one hit record with "Heartbreak Hotel"	1957
Neil Armstrong, commander of *Apollo 11*, becomes first astronaut to walk on the moon	1969
Richard M. Nixon resigns as president of the United States	1974

BIBLIOGRAPHY

Buchoholz, Elke Linda. Zimmermann, Beate. Ullmann, H.F. **Pablo Picasso: Life and Work**. Konemann, Germany, 2008.

Green, Jen; Hughes, Andrew S.; Mason, Antony. **Famous Artists: Picasso**. Barrons, New York, 1995.

Heslewood, Juliet. **Introducing Picasso**. Little, Brown and Company, New York, 1993.

Kelley, True (Illustrator). **Pablo Picasso: Breaking All the Rules**. Penguin Group (USA), New York, 2002.

Leslie, Richard. **Pablo Picasso: A Modern Master**. New Line Books, New York, 2006.

Meadows, Matthew. **Art for Young People: Pablo Picasso**. Sterling Publishing, New York, 1996.

Scarborough, Kate. **Artists in Their Time: Pablo Picasso**. Children's Press, New York, 2002.

Schaffner, Ingrid. **Essential Pablo Picasso**. Harry Abrams, Inc. New York, 1999.

Warncke, Carsten-Peter. **Picasso**. Taschen, London, 1998.

Wertenbaker, Lael. **The World of Picasso 1881-1973**. Time-Life Books, New York, 1974.